THIS GUIDE BELONGS TO

AS THEY PARENT

Date / Year

Kind Words from Parents, Grandparents, & Experts in Parenting

Sandra Stanley

Author of *Breathing Room*, and co-author of *Parenting: Getting it Right*, foster care advocate, mother of three

We all know where we want to end up in our parenting, but how to get there can seem like an unsolved mystery. The *Phase Guides* give us a resource to help out. They help to guide parents and caregivers through the different seasons of raising children, and provide a road map to parenting in such a way that we finish up with very few regrets.

Sissy Goff M.Ed., LPC-MHSP

Co-director of Child and Adolescent Counseling at Daystar Counseling Ministries, speaker and author of 12 books, including *Brave*

It's hard to connect with your child without first understanding where they are. As counselors and speakers at parenting events across the country, we spend a great deal of time teaching parents about development. To know where your child is—not just physically, but emotionally, socially, and spiritually, helps you to truly know and understand who your child is. And that understanding is the key to connecting.

The *Phase Guides* give you the tools to do just that. Through the research of the Phase Project, *Phase Guides* are an insightful, hopeful, practical, and literal year-by-year guide that will help you to understand and connect with your child at every age.

Jennifer Walker, RN BSN

Author and co-founder of Moms On Call, mother of three

These resources for parents are fantastically empowering, absolute in their simplicity, and completely doable in every way. The hard work that has gone into the Phase Project will echo through the next generation of children in powerful ways.

Tina Naidoo

Executive Director of The Potter's House of Dallas, Inc

It's true that parenting is one of life's greatest joys but it is not without its challenges. If we're honest, parenting can sometimes feel like trying to choreograph a dance to an ever-changing beat. It can be clumsy and riddled with well-meaning missteps. If parenting is a dance, this *Phase Guide* is a skilled instructor refining your technique and helping you move gracefully to a steady beat.

For those of us who love to plan ahead, this guide will help you anticipate what's to come so you can be poised and ready to embrace the moments you want to enjoy.

Carlos Whittaker

Speaker, storyteller, best-selling author of multiple books, including *How to Human*, father of three

Not only are the *Phase Guides* the most creative and well-thought-out guides to parenting I have ever encountered, these books are essential to my daily parenting.

With three kids of my own, I know what it's like to swim in the wake of daily drama and delicacy. These books are a reminder to enjoy every second. Because it's just a phase.

Cheryl Jackson

Founder of Minnie's Food Pantry, award-winning philanthropist, grandmother

As the founder of Minnie's Food Pantry, I see thousands of people each month with children who will benefit from the advice, guidance, and nuggets of information on how to celebrate and understand the phases of their child's life.

Too often we feel like we're losing our mind when sweet little Johnny starts to change his behavior into a person we do not know. I can't wait to start implementing the principles of these books with my clients to remind them... it's just a phase.

David Thomas, LMSW

Co-director of Family Counseling, Daystar Counseling Ministries, speaker, and author of 10 Books including *Wild Things: The Art of Nurturing Boys*, father of three

I began exploring this resource with my counselor hat on, thinking how valuable this will be for the many parents I spend time with in my office. I ended up taking my counselor hat off and putting on my parent hat. Then I kept thinking about friends who are teachers, coaches, youth pastors, and children's ministers, who would want this in their hands.

What a valuable resource the Orange team has given us to better understand and care for the kids and adolescents we love. I look forward to sharing it broadly.

Josh Shipp

Best-selling author of *The Grown-Up's Guide to Teenage Humans*, award-winning speaker, teen expert, father of three

As I speak to high school students and their parents, I always wonder to myself: What would it have been like if they had better seen what was coming next? What if they had a guide that would tell them what to expect and how to be ready? What if they could anticipate what is predictable about the high school years before they actually hit?

These *Phase Guides* give a parent that kind of preparation so they can have a plan when they need it most.

Danielle Strickland

Speaker, global social activist, author of *The Other Side of Hope*, mother of three

The *Phase Guides* are incredibly creative, well researched, and filled with inspirational actions for everyday life. Each age-specific guide is catalytic for equipping parents to lead and love their kids as they grow up.

I'm blown away and deeply encouraged by the content and by its creators. I highly recommend Phase resources for all parents, teachers, and influencers of children. This is the stuff that challenges us and changes our world. Get them. Read them. And use them!

Courtney DeFeo

Author of *Treasured* and *In This House* and *We Will Giggle*, podcaster, mother of two

I have always wished someone would hand me a manual for parenting. Well, the *Phase Guides* are more than what I wished for. They guide, inspire, and challenge me as a parent—while giving me incredible insight into my children at each age and phase. Our family will be using these every year!

PARENT CUE

Parenting Your Two-Year-Old

A GUIDE TO MAKING THE MOST OF
THE "I CAN DO IT" PHASE

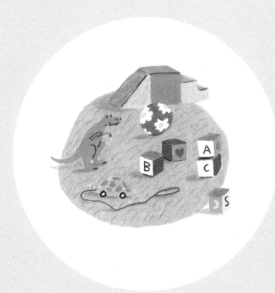

THE PHASE PROJECT

Parenting Your Two-Year-Old:
A Guide to Making the Most of the
"I Can Do It" Phase

Published by Orange, a division of The reThink Group, Inc.,
5870 Charlotte Lane, Suite 300, Cumming, GA 30040 U.S.A.

Parent Cue ® is a registered trademark of The reThink Group, Inc.
It's Just a Phase ® is a registered trademark of The Phase Project, LLC.

ISBN: 978-1-63570-215-6
© 2024 The Phase Project, LLC

Printed in United States of America
Second Edition 2024
1 2 3 4 5 6 7 8 9 10
06/01/2024

Special thanks to —

JON ACUFF for guidance and consultation on having conversations about technological responsibility

JIM BURNS, PH.D for guidance and consultation on having conversations about sexual integrity

JEAN SUMNER, MD for guidance and consultation on having conversations about healthy habits

CHINWÉ WILLIAMS, PH.D for guidance and consultation on how to navigate crisis

Every educator, counselor, community leader, and researcher who invested in the Phase Project

In Partnership →

Parent Cue partners with the Phase Project, designing Phase Guides to help you parent your child through every year in the four main phases: Preschool, Elementary School, Middle School, and High School.

The Phase Project →

Started in 2013, the Phase Project is a synthesis of personal experience, academic research, and gatherings of leaders and educational experts from across the child development spectrum.

Contents

How to Use This Guide

The guide you hold in your hand doesn't have very many words, but it does have a lot of ideas.

Some of these ideas come from thousands of hours of research. Others come from parents, educators, and volunteers who spend every day with kids the same age as yours. This guide won't tell you everything about your kid, but it will tell you a few things about kids at this age.

The best way to use this guide is to take what these pages tell you about two-year-olds and combine it with what you know is true about your two-year-old.

After each idea in this guide, there are pages with a few questions designed to prompt you to think about your kid, your family, and yourself as a parent. The only guarantee we give to parents who use this guide is this: You will mess up some things as a parent this year. Actually, that's a guarantee to every parent, regardless. But you, you picked up this book!

You want to be a better parent. And that's what we hope this guide will do: help you parent your toddler just a little better, simply because you paused to consider a few ideas that can help you make the most of this phase.

Let's sum it up:

Things about two-year-olds

+

Thoughts about your two-year-old

=

Your guide to the next 52 weeks of parenting

Dear Parent,

Welcome to a new phase!

LIFE CAN BE CHALLENGING AND UNPREDICTABLE. And, if you're parenting a two-year-old, you're guaranteed this year will have plenty of both. That sweet baby who used to cuddle in your arms has not only learned how to walk, but now he can run away from you—and fast. That little angel whose smile used to light up your world can now smile at you as she drops your phone—*into the bathtub*.

Personally, I've raised two men who have given me four beautiful grandchildren all currently under the age of six years old. I've seen enough to know the phrase "terrible twos" wasn't invented without reason. There are days in this phase when "terrible" may seem like the only word to characterize the state of your home, your schedule, and your patience. This is the phase when a toddler suddenly explodes with personality.

It's the moment they fall to the floor screaming because you cut their sandwich the wrong way. Or you bring them the milk they asked for, and they realize they really wanted orange juice. Or you tell them they aren't allowed to do that completely irrational thing they were just trying to do, and the world suddenly falls apart. Yes, you will have moments this year when you stare, wide-eyed, at the determined child in front of you and wonder: *What am I supposed to do with this?*

The answer, even though it may not seem true in the moment, is really what it has always been: love. Becoming a grandparent has heightened my senses to my grandchildren's need for love. It's funny, the way time gives us perspective. Love is the thing every selfish, stubborn, crazy-headed toddler needs most.

I remember when my grandson Amari was two, he told me he loved me for the first time. Each time he said it, he put his whole body into it. It was like he couldn't say it loud enough or strong enough. He just had to let me know that HE LOVED ME!

One day, as I was leaving his house, we started a back-and-forth shouting match to tell each other how much we loved each other. It was so passionate and so pure that I took out my cell phone and recorded him on video. Within days after sharing it on social media, over 26 million people had watched, commented, and shared the video. The video was shown on *Good Morning America* and *The Ellen Show.*

I know most people's toddler videos don't make national television. But that's not the point. The point is there's something about the love of a two-year-old that can capture the heart of a nation. And that love is inside your child, too.

Sure, this year your toddler is becoming more independent. But that means when she shows you love and affection, she does it because she chooses to. When he tells you he loves you, he says it because *he means it*. And as the parent of a two-year-old, you'll discover you have more love inside you than you ever knew possible. It's a shouting-match kind of love that will see you through the tantrums. It's a love that may catch you off guard as you find yourself captivated by this adorable, growing, bundle of personality.

Cheryl Jackson

Founder of Minnie's Food Pantry, award-winning philanthropist, and grandmother

52 Weeks to Parent Your Two-Year-Old

WHEN YOU See
HOW MUCH TiME
YOU HAVE LeFT,
YOU TeND TO DO
MORE WiTH
THE TiME YOU
HAVE NOW.

For some, this phase sounds like...

● words they may say
○ words you may say

Read it AGAIN!

Please don't give up your nap yet.

That's not a toy.

I do it myself.

I no want it. No, I want it!

Why are you naked?

Mine.

Boogers don't go on the floor.

Psghetti.

Can I eat a marshpillow?

Use your inside voice.

My bulzodor!

Play with me.

Why are you so sticky?

There are approximately 936 weeks from the time a baby is born until they grow up and move to whatever is next.

It may seem hard to believe, but at least 104 of those weeks have already passed you by. And, while the future still feels far away, you're probably beginning to realize that your toddler is growing up faster than you ever dreamed.

That's why every week counts. Of course, each week on its own might not feel significant. There may be weeks this year when you feel like all you've accomplished was enduring an epic toddler tantrum. That's okay.

Take a deep breath. You don't have to get everything done this week.

But what happens in your child's life week after week, year after year, adds up over time. So, it might be a good idea to put a number to your weeks.

Measure It Out

If you want a little help counting it out, you can download the free Parent Cue app on all mobile platforms.

Write down the number of weeks that have already passed since your two-year-old was born. Then write down the number of weeks you have left before they graduate high school.

Write down the number.

Create a Visual Countdown

Find a jar and fill it with one marble for each week you have remaining with your child. Then make a habit of removing one marble every week as a reminder to make the most of your time.

Where can you place your visual countdown so you will see it frequently?

Which day of the week is best for you to remove a marble?

Is there anything you want to do each week as you remove a marble?

HINT:

Say a prayer, write in a baby book, retell one favorite memory from this past week.

Bonus idea— place the marble you removed into a second jar so you can see how much time you've invested in your child.

You only have <u>52 weeks</u> with your two-year-old while they are still two.

Then they will be three, and you will never know them as a two-year-old again. That might be incredibly emotional, or it might be the best news you've heard all day.

Or to say it another way:

> **Before you know it, your toddler will grow up a little more and...**
> → **be potty trained.**
> → **speak clearly.**
> → **blow their own nose.**

Just remember, the phase you are in now has remarkable potential. Before their third birthday, there are some distinctive opportunities you don't want to miss.

So, as you count down the next 52 weeks, pay attention to what makes these weeks different from the rest of the weeks you will have with your child as they grow.

EVERY PHASE IS A TIMEFRAME IN A KID OR TEENAGER'S LIFE WHEN YOU CAN LEVERAGE DISTINCTIVE OPPORTUNITIES TO INFLUENCE THEIR FUTURE.

Reflect

What are some things you have noticed about your two-year-old in this phase that you really enjoy?

What is something new you are learning as a parent during this phase?

The phase when nobody's on time, everything's a mess, and one eager toddler will insist, "I can do it."

Expect to be late.

Maybe you had to wait for your toddler to "do it myself" (just try and stop them). Or maybe they impressively filled a clean diaper just as you got into the car. Whatever the reason, this phase will make even the most punctual adult miss the mark occasionally.

Look forward to a few fashion statements.

Expect a few mismatched outfits, magic marker tattoos, sticker collages, and other various states of creative expression. In this phase, you will choose not only your battles, but also which messes will just have to be tolerated.

Their struggle for independence has begun.

Your first clue might be your toddler's three new favorite words: "me," "myself," and "I." Just remember, by letting them do some things "myself," they're not only learning new skills, they're also developing the confidence they need in order to move to the next phase.

Every two-year-old is unique.

Even with unique two-year-olds—which yours most certainly is—most two-year-olds have a few things in common. This book will show you what those are so you can make the most of the "I Can Do It" Phase.

Remember: We haven't met your two-year-old. This book is just about a lot of two-year-olds.

Some may still be working on their first words.

Some will never. Stop. Talking.

Some will always poop in the big toilet.

Some may prefer to smear their diapers on the wall.

Some will happily eat quinoa and artichokes.

Some will go on hunger strike if it's not a chicken nugget.

Some will model cute hats all day long.

Some will remove their socks and shoes in eleven seconds flat.

Some take a two-hour nap every afternoon.

Some have to be barricaded in their room for a ten-minute quiet time.

Some can climb up and down the stairs without help.

Some are climbing up the walls.

Some may craft amazing shapes from Play-Doh.®

Some may eat the Play-Doh.® (Okay, so we're pretty sure all of them do that.)

This year, your two-year-old is changing.

YEARS	2	2½	3

Physically

Jumps in place

Throws a ball overhead

Briefly stands on one foot

May demonstrate hand preference

Mentally

Follows simple instructions

Benefits from repetition

Is unable to take the point of view of other people

Learns through engaging their five senses

YEARS	2	2½	3

Verbally

Says 40-50 words including some action words like, "Go"

approximately 300 words and simple sentences like "I do it."

Learns how to whisper

Understands more than they can communicate

Emotionally

May begin to bite, scream, and throw tantrums

Plays next to, rather than with, playmates

Recognizes basic emotions in others

May begin to name their own emotions like, "I'm happy."

What are some changes you are noticing in your two-year-old?

You may disagree with some of the characteristics we've shared about two-year-olds. That's because every two-year-old is unique.

What makes your two-year-old different from two-year-olds in general?

What do you want to remember about this year with your two-year-old?

HINT:

There are enough lines for at least one per week. Throughout the year, write down a few simple things you want to remember.

Potty Training

Milestone moments like this one may raise anxiety for both you and your child. To help you prepare, here are a few practical suggestions:

Start when they are ready. Most toddlers are ready to potty train between 27 and 32 months. Your toddler may be ready to begin when...

→ diaper stays dry for at least two hours
→ can tell (or show) you when they need to go
→ bothered when diaper is dirty
→ can pull their pants off and back on
→ can understand and follow directions

Celebrate! Whether you make a chart for stickers or do a potty dance, make sure to celebrate the successes—no matter how small.

Prepare for accidents. Accidents will happen. Keep extra clothes on hand and help your toddler not to feel ashamed by letting him know, "Accidents happen, and that's okay."

Keep the nighttime diaper. Let them experience daytime success before tackling the nighttime. Taking on too much too fast will only discourage you both.

Reflect

What are some tricks you want to try when you and your toddler are ready to potty train?

What is your plan for how to handle accidents?

Six Things Every Kid Needs

WHEN YOU see HOW MUCH TiMe YOU HAVe LeFT, YOU TeND TO MAKE WHAT MATTeRS, MATTeR MORe.

It's worth repeating: When you see how much time you have left, you tend to make what matters, matter more.

Depending on your personality, that can sound empowering, or just like a lot of pressure. Relax. Every day doesn't have to create a memory worth posting.

The important thing to remember is a countdown clock doesn't mean you try to squeeze more things into each week so you can get the most out of it. It actually means acknowledging that you can't do what you can't do.

You can't make your toddler always behave in public. But over time you can show them the kind of love that is the foundation for how we treat each other.

You can't make your toddler make wise choices. But over time you can introduce them to stories that widen their perspective and inform their decision-making.

You can't make your toddler be a good friend. But you can give them safe places to belong so they will know that people matter.

You can't make your toddler perform at the top of their class. But you can make learning fun, and use mistakes as opportunities to grow.

This week matters because it's an opportunity to give your toddler a few things that really matter. You can't do what you can't do. Let some things go, and you might just discover you're already doing more significant things than you ever realized.

Your kid needs
six things over time.

Over the next 832 weeks, your child will need many things.

Some of the things your kid needs will change from phase to phase, but there are six things that every kid needs at every phase. In fact, these things may be the most important things you give your kid— other than food. Kids need food.

The next few pages are designed to help you think about how you can give these things to your two-year-old—before they turn three.

Every kid, at every phase, needs:

 Love to give them a sense of *worth*.

 Stories to give them a bigger *perspective*.

 Work to give them *purpose*.

 Fun to give them *connection*.

 People to give them *belonging*.

 Words to give them *direction*.

No. 1

Every kid needs **love** over time to give them a sense of **worth.**

**One question your
two-year-old is asking:**

Your toddler's changing ability is a crisis—for you,
and for them. This is a season filled with uncertainty,
imperfection, and even failure as they struggle to keep
up with all their newly developing skills. Your two-year-
old is asking one major question: **"Am I able?"**

As the parent of a two-year-old who may scream more
than you imagined, sleep less than you had hoped, or
make more messes than you thought possible, you may
feel overwhelmed at times. But remember this—in order
to give your two-year-old the love they need, you only
need to do one thing: **Embrace their physical needs.**

When you embrace your two-year-old's physical needs, you...
① communicate that they are safe,
② establish that the world can be trusted, and
③ demonstrate that they are worth loving.

Reflect

You are probably doing more than you realize to show your two-year-old just how much you love them.

Make a list of the ways you already show up consistently to embrace your two-year-old's physical needs.

Showing love requires paying attention to what someone likes.

What does your two-year-old seem to enjoy the most right now?

It's impossible to love anyone with the relentless effort a two-year-old demands unless you have a little time for yourself.

What can you do to refuel each week so you are able to give your two-year-old the love they need?

Who do you have around you supporting you this year?

No. 2

Every kid needs **stories** over time to give them a bigger **perspective.**

02 / 06

Books to read with your two-year-old:

Ten Black Dots
by Donald Crews

Full, Full, Full of Love
by Trish Cooke

Llama, Llama *(series)*
by Anna Dewdney

Are You My Mother?
by P.D. Eastman

Go, Dog. Go!
by P.D. Eastman

I Want That
by Hannah Eliot

Everyone Poops
by Taro Gomi

5 Minutes to Bedtime:
An Ollie Adventure
by Liz Hansen

The Snowy Day
by Ezra Jack Keats

One Love
by Bob Marley

A Fly Went
by Mike McClintock

Blueberries for Sal
by Robert McCloskey

If You Give a Mouse
a Cookie
by Laura Joffe Numeroff

Bunny Days
by Tao Nyeu

All Are Welcome
by Alexandra Penfold

Goodnight, Goodnight,
Construction Site
by Sheri Duskey Rinker

Sheep in a Jeep
by Nancy E. Shaw

Even Firefighters Go to
the Potty
by Wendy Way and Naomi Wax

Don't Let the Pigeon
Drive the Bus
by Mo Willems

HINT:
*You can find a
more in-depth
reading list at
ParentCue.org.*

Reflect

Kids need the kind of stories you will read to them over time. But they also need family stories.

HINT:

Remember to look at this list throughout the year to continue to capture your family's story.

What can you do this year to capture your family's story so you can retell the story of this year to your two-year-old when they are older?

JOURNAL

What makes your family history unique? How can you preserve the story of your family's history for your two-year-old?

Are there other stories that matter to you? What are they, and how will you share those stories with your toddler?

No. 3

Every kid needs **work** over time to give them **purpose.**

Work your two-year-old can do:

Pick up a toy and put it away

Hold a sippy cup

Drink from a straw

Take trash to the trash can

Follow two-step instructions

Help fill a pet's food dish

Help as you dress them
(by holding out arms, legs, or feet)

Undress themselves

Feed themselves

Clean up spills

Sleep in a toddler bed
(most of the time)

Use the potty
(maybe)

Reflect

What are some things your two-year-old has worked to accomplish so far?

Letting your two-year-old "do it myself" takes patience—and a lot of wet wipes.

How are you allowing for extra time for your two-year-old to try new things?
What do you do to reward their efforts?

What are some things you hope your two-year-old will be able to do independently in the next phase?

How are you helping your two-year-old develop those skills now?

No. 4

Every kid needs **fun** over time to give them **connection.**

Ways to have fun with your two-year-old:

Toys ●
Activities ●

Push a swing

Alphabet blocks

Roll a ball

Trucks & trains & dolls

Peg puzzles & pounding bench

Play kitchen

Do a silly dance

Bead mazes

Go to the park

A soft ball for throwing & rolling

Jumbo crayons

Play-Doh®

Blow bubbles

Sing "Itsy-Bitsy-Spider"

Riding & scooting toys

Finger paint

Let them "hide"

Mega Blocks®

Reflect

What are some activities that make you and your two-year-old laugh?

When are the best times of the day, or week, for you to set aside to have fun
with your two-year-old?

What are some ways you want to celebrate the special days coming up this year?

Third Birthday

Holidays

No. 5

Every kid needs **people** over time to give them **belonging.**

Adults who might influence your two-year-old:

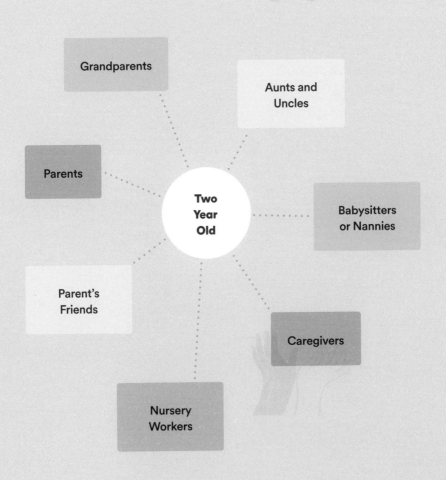

Grandparents

Aunts and Uncles

Parents

Two Year Old

Babysitters or Nannies

Parent's Friends

Caregivers

Nursery Workers

Reflect

HINT:
They're probably the adults who understand some of your two-year-old's words.

List at least five adults who have influence in your two-year-old's life right now.

What is one way these adults could help you and your two-year-old this year?

EXAMPLES:

Pray for you, read to your two-year-old, give your two-year-old an opportunity to play with another kid

What are a few ways you could show these adults appreciation for the significant role they play in your child's life?

No. 6

Every kid needs **words** over time to give them **direction.**

Words your two-year-old needs to hear:

I love you!

You're okay.

Good morning!

You did it!

Thank you.

Excuse me.

Please.

You're welcome.

Be gentle.

I will be back.

I'm sorry.

Good night!

Improving your child's vocabulary will help them in the phases to come. Here are a few ways you can help:

① Talk to your toddler—the more, the better.

② Use facial expressions and body language often.

③ Repeat what they say, and add words. (When they say "truck," you say, "Would you like to play with your truck?")

④ Give your toddler options. ("Do you want an apple or a banana?")

Reflect

What word (or words) describe your hopes for your two-year-old in this phase?

Determined	Motivated	Gentle
Encouraging	Introspective	Passionate
Self-Assured	Enthusiastic	Patient
Assertive	Joyful	Forgiving
Daring	Entertaining	Creative
Insightful	Independent	Witty
Compassionate	Observant	Ambitious
Amiable	Sensitive	Helpful
Easy-Going	Endearing	Authentic
Diligent	Adventurous	Inventive
Proactive	Honest	Devoted
Optimistic	Curious	Genuine
Fearless	Dependable	Attentive
Affectionate	Generous	Harmonious
Courageous	Committed	Empathetic
Cautious	Responsible	Courageous
Devoted	Trustworthy	Flexible
Inquisitive	Thoughtful	Careful
Patient	Loyal	Nurturing
Open-minded	Kind	Reliable

Where can you place those words in your home so they will remind you what you want for your two-year-old this year?

HINT:

At some point this year, try to get a recording of their voice—it will have changed before you know it.

Write down some of your two-year-old's first sentences or favorite words.

WHEN YOU see
HOW MUCH TIME
YOU HAVE LEFT,
YOU TeND TO VALUE
WHAT HAPPeNS
OVER TIMe.

The most important things we give our kids aren't the gifts we just give once, but the ones we give over time. Just remember...

We don't experience worth because we are loved once, but because we are **loved** by someone over time.

We don't understand the world through a single event, but through a collection of **stories** over time.

We don't usually discover our purpose in one great revelation, but through consistent opportunities to **work** over time.

We don't develop trusted relationships in a day, but we become connected to others through laughter, **fun**, and shared experiences over time.

We don't know we belong because of a single invitation, but because we have been welcomed by **people** over time.

We are not motivated to action by one statement, but by **words** that move us over time.

Four Conversations to Have in this Phase

WHEN YOU KNOW WHERE YOU WANT TO GO, AND YOU KNOW WHERE YOU ARE NOW, YOU CAN ALWAYS DO SOMETHING TO MOVE IN A BETTER DIRECTION.

Over the next 832 weeks of your child's life, some conversations may matter more than others.

What you say, for example, regarding **pirates, spiders, and football** might have less impact on their future than what you say regarding **health, sex, technology, or faith.**

The next pages are about the conversations that matter most. On the left page is a destination—what you might want to be true in your kid's life 832 weeks from now. On the right page is a goal for conversations with your two-year-old and a few suggestions about what you might want to say.

Healthy Habits

Learning to strengthen my body through exercise, nutrition, and self-advocacy

This year you will establish basic nutrition so your child will have consistent care and experience a variety of food.

Even though you no longer have pediatric visits every few months, you should schedule a well visit at least once per year. You can also begin to build a foundation of healthy habits for your two-year-old with a few simple words.

Say things like...

Time to brush your teeth!

It's nap time.

Here's your milk.

Let's go outside.

Let's wash your hands.

Reflect

HINT:
Okay,
"exercise" may
be a stretch,
but running
after big kids
at the park
counts.

What are your goals for providing your two-year-old with good nutrition and exercise?

Who will help you monitor and improve your two-year-old's health this year?

What are your own health goals for this year? How can you improve the habits in your own life—even in a phase when you might find yourself asking, "Should I eat that mac 'n' cheese they hardly touched?"

Sexual Integrity

Guarding my potential for intimacy through appropriate boundaries and mutual respect

This year you will <u>introduce them to their body</u> so your child will discover their body and define privacy.

There's a good chance your two-year-old is becoming more aware of their body and the bodies of others. Use this time to lay a foundation for future conversations by simply talking about bodies in a positive way.

Say things like...

...

That's your nose. Those are your eyes. That's your vagina/penis.

Help your child learn the correct names of body parts—experts suggest that learning proper words can protect your kid from potential harm as well as create a positive view of their body.

...

No, girls don't have a penis.

If your child notices that someone's body is different than their own, talk about the difference.

Reflect

HINT:

Parents,
media, friends,
other adults…

What influences shaped your views of sex growing up?

How does your own life story shape your future hopes for your child in this area?

When it comes to your child's sexuality, what do you hope is true for them 832 weeks from now?

Are you and your spouse, or your child's other parent, on the same page when it comes to talking about sex with your child?

How might you work on a plan to communicate your hopes and expectations about sex through real-time conversations with your child?

Technological Responsibility

Leveraging the potential of online experiences to enhance my offline community and success

This year you will enjoy the advantages so your child will experience boundaries and have positive exposure.

One advantage to technology is that you probably already have a resident expert who navigates a tablet faster than some adults. But since two-year-olds are drawn to a screen, it's also time to have a few conversations about digital devices.

Say things like...

Look at you!

Take as many photos as you like. You will enjoy seeing them later.

A phone is not a hammer.

Tablets don't go in the bathtub.

No juice by the computer.

Let's turn off the TV now.

Two-year-olds don't need to watch a full season of *Sesame Street* in one sitting.

Reflect

What kind of digital access was available to you when you were growing up?
How have things changed since then?

What are some issues you think may come up as you raise your two-year-old in a digitally connected world? Where can you go to find advice to help navigate those issues?

When it comes to your child's engagement with technology, what do you hope is true for them 832 weeks from now?

What are your own personal values and disciplines when it comes to leveraging technology? Are there ways you want to improve your own savvy, skill, or responsibility in this area?

Authentic Faith

Trusting Jesus in a way
that transforms how I love
God, myself, and the rest
of the world

This year you will incite wonder so your child
will know God's love and meet God's family.

Your two-year-old listens to your words.
So this phase is the perfect time to begin
talking, singing, and reading out loud with
your toddler about faith. Begin by simply
incorporating faith into your daily routines.

Say things like...

God made you. God loves you.
Jesus wants to be your friend forever.

God, thank You for...
God, please help us...

Pray aloud while you are with
your two-year-old.

Jesus loves me.

Sing songs together.

Let's read about how God made
the world. Let's read about Christmas.
Let's read about Easter.

Read a few Bible story books—
the kind with really good pictures.

Reflect

Who will help you develop your child's faith as they grow?

Is there a volunteer at your church who shows up consistently each week for your child? Do you attend a consistent service so your two-year-old knows who will greet them each week?

When it comes to your child's faith, what do you hope is true for them 832 weeks from now?

What routines or habits do you have in your own life that are stretching your faith?

Rhythms and Responses

The rhythm of your week will shape the values in your home.

Now that you have filled this book with dreams, ideas, and goals, it may seem as if you will never have time to get it all done. Actually, you have 832 weeks. And every week has potential.

The secret to making the most of this phase with your two-year-old is to take advantage of the time you already have. Create a rhythm to your weeks by leveraging these four times together.

Morning Time

Set the mood for the day. Smile. Greet them with words of love.

Drive Time

Reinforce simple ideas. Talk to your toddler and play music as you go.

Cuddle Time

Be personal. Spend one-on-one time that communicates love and affection.

Bath Time

Wind down together. Provide comfort as the day draws to a close.

Reflect

What seem to be your two-year-old's best times of the day?

What are some of your favorite routines with your two-year-old?

Write down any other thoughts or questions that you have about parenting your two-year-old.

Preparing for the Unexpected

Parenting humans at any phase of life is filled with the unexpected.

No matter the age, sometimes the unexpected discoveries we make as parents may elicit fear, anger, or confusion as we try to guide our kid toward a positive future. It may even be something that is completely out of our control, like a medical diagnosis or a family tragedy. That's why it's best to create a response plan when you are clear and thoughtful.

So, take a few, deep breaths. Find a place where you feel safe and comfortable. If you need to walk away and come back to this at a later time, that's okay, too.

Download → parentcue.org/preparing

Reflect

Every parent has what it takes to navigate challenges with their kids, but none of us can carry the weight alone.

Think of someone with whom you feel safe enough to be completely honest about what is happening and what you are feeling.

JOURNAL

If you were to discover something you weren't expecting in your kid's life, who would you be able to call?

How would you begin that conversation?

Every kid who is navigating challenging situations needs their parent's involvement. But a parent may not be the only influence they need.

If you were to discover something you weren't expecting, who else in your kid's life could you count on to walk with them through this experience?

HINT:

Think of someone who shares your values.

_____

_____

_____

_____

_____

What might you want to go ahead and share with them about your kid and/ or your family?

_____

_____

_____

_____

_____

_____

_____

Navigating Crisis

What is a crisis?

A crisis is any real or perceived threat to your child. And it's inevitable. Even though you are a great parent, you won't be able to protect your child from some pain during their preschool years. There is a wide range of events that classify as "crisis" ranging from temporary to long-term and from mild to severe.

How do you recognize it?

Just because your preschooler may not know how to talk about it doesn't mean they are unaffected. Watch for these three things:

① Are they regressing?

During a crisis, preschoolers will often try to take more control of their world by regressing in potty training, verbal skills, motor development, or behavior.

② How are they playing?

As your preschooler plays with toys, listen to the conversations the toys have with each other and watch how the toys treat each other.

③ What are they drawing?

Preschoolers may begin to draw what they are processing. Asking your child about their drawings will give you insight into their mind and heart.

How do you respond to it?

① Re-establish some routine.

Preschoolers love predictability. Talk to them about changes in their routine while reminding them what has stayed the same. Establish new expectations and a new routine.

② Play with them.

If you notice something in your child's play, join them. Thirty minutes of one-on-one play with your child establishes a meaningful connection, which helps them feel safe.

③ Make music.

Music is healing. It's multi-sensory, non-threatening, structured, personalized, fun, and accessible.

④ Respect their boundaries.

When offering affection, model and respect their boundaries by asking, "Would you like me to hold you?" "Do you want a hug?" Your preschooler may need a safe space alone to process their emotions first.

⑤ Answer their questions.

Listen first. Paraphrase their words to make sure you understand their question and concern. Then, give an honest answer in a calm, reassuring voice, using as few words as possible.

⑥ **Take care of yourself.**

When your preschooler is in crisis, you may be in crisis as well. Seek care. Find community. Take some personal time. This may be the best thing you can do to help your child.

⑦ **Get outside help.**

Consider if your preschooler is being hurt by someone, hurting others, or hurting themselves. Or if you are also hurting and not currently able to provide support.

What's Next: The Three-Year-Old Phase

In only 52 weeks you will rediscover your toddler as a three-year-old.

One of the joys of parenting is the many surprises that greet you around every corner.

We can't prepare you for all the joys that await you in the next phase, but we can give you a glimpse of a few things that might help you anticipate what's coming.

The three-year-old phase may look like...

Playing dress-up

Laughing at their attempts at telling a joke

Making everything into a game

Convincing them they want to do things they really don't want to do

Switching the crib out to a big kid bed

Hiding the scissors so they don't cut their own hair

Waiting too long while they put on their own shoes

Meltdowns in the grocery store

Trying to answer the incessant "why" question

In not so many weeks you may discover an emerging three-year-old who is ready to start asking you, **"Why?"**

Three-Year-Old

The phase when anything can be imagined, everything can be a game, and one curious preschooler wants to know, *"Why?"*

Imagination is reality.

Your three-year-old might suddenly become a self-proclaimed princess, pirate, or superhero. Your bedroom might turn out to be a train station, a castle, or both. But imagination may also turn scary. Fear may set in when, at any given moment, a monster can show up in the hallway, a snake can be under the bed, or a dragon can walk through the living room.

Everything can be a game.

You motivate your preschooler best when you appeal to their desire to play. Whatever the task, turn it into a game; make it fun. When you're having fun, they'll have fun with you. And there is simply nothing more entertaining than the spontaneous laughter of a three-year-old.

They have a newfound curiosity.

Whether it's showcased in unrolling the toilet paper, pulling apart an older kid's LEGOs®, or the constant repetition of "Why? Why? Why?", your preschooler is eager to know how the world works. So when they ask you "Why?" for the second and third time, remember they're just looking for more of the knowledge they know you must have.

The Phase Timeline

HINT:

The full Phase Timeline is available at parentcue.org/ timeline.

About the Timeline

The one thing that is true across every phase is that your child will change—and so will your role as a parent. The phase timeline is a visual to help you see the progression through their first 18 years. Reference it over time to remember where you have been and to get an idea of where you are heading.

About the Curve

Your child will also experience different levels of intensity across the phases. Watch for where the line rises to know when your child may be experiencing more developmental intensity. Whenever that seems overwhelming, this timeline is a reminder that it's just a phase.

Remember: We haven't met your kid. This timeline is just what's true for a lot of kids.

Preschool → **Your role is to embrace their physical needs.**

↓

Elementary School → **Your role is to engage their interests.**

↓

Middle School → **Your role is to affirm their personal journey.**

↓

High School → **Your role is to mobilize their potential.**

The Preschool Phase

Your Role →

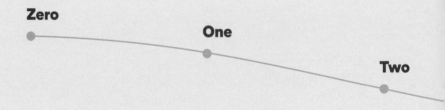

Embrace their physical needs.

Zero

One

Two

New Baby

Wants to know...

Am I safe?

So...

Establish trust.

One-Year-Old & Two-Year-Old

Wants to know...

Am I able?

So...

Develop their confidence.

Thinks Like →

A preschooler thinks like an artist, so engage with their senses.

Motivated By →

A preschooler is motivated by safety, so respond consistently.

Three

Four

Three-Year-Old & Four-Year-Old

Wants to know...

Am I okay?

So...

Cultivate their self-control.

It's just a phase, so don't miss it.

JOURNAL

Be the parent you want to be with Parent Cue.

We believe in every parent's ability to be the parent their child needs. Good parenting takes on many forms!

Parent Cue is here to cue you with what you need, when you need it—curated content, weekly inspiration, free resources, products, and more—so you are equipped to be the parent you want to be.

Get started → parentcue.org

Parent smarter, not harder.

Make the most of everyday moments on the go. Download the free Parent Cue app to get weekly cues and content to connect with your kid in every phase from New Baby to Twelfth Grade—available for iOS and Android. Weekly phase content also available with an in-app subscription.

Download now → parentcue.org/app

Ready for the next phase.

These guides are the core product of the Phase Project—a synthesis of personal experience, academic research, and gatherings of leaders and educational experts from across the child development spectrum.

Just like this one, each guide will help you make the most of every phase in your child's life through:

① What is changing about your kid
② The six things your kid needs most
③ Four conversations to have each year
④ Rhythms and responses
⑤ What's next

A guide for every phase.

This guide is one of an eighteen-part series, so you can follow your parenting journey across every phase from New Baby to Twelfth Grade.

Preschool Phase	Elementary School Phase	Middle School Phase	High School Phase
New Baby The "I need you now" Phase	**Kindergartner** The "Look at me!" Phase	**Sixth Grader** The "Who Cares" Phase	**Ninth Grader** The "This is Me Now" Phase
One-Year-Old The "I can do it" Phase	**First Grader** The "Look at me!" Phase	**Seventh Grader** The "Who's Going?" Phase	**Tenth Grader** The "Why not?" Phase
Two-Year-Old The "I can do it" Phase	**Second Grader** The "Sounds like fun!" Phase	**Eighth Grader** The "Yeah... I Know" Phase	**Eleventh Grader** The "Just Trust Me" Phase
Three-Year-Old The "Why?" Phase	**Third Grader** The "Sounds like fun!" Phase		**Twelfth Grader** The "What's Next?" Phase
Four-Year-Old The "Why?" Phase	**Fourth Grader** The "I've Got This" Phase		
	Fifth Grader The "I've Got This" Phase		

Shop now → phaseguides.com